Rich or Poor?

Written by Lynette Evans
Illustrated by Mike Spoor

Brazil

My name is Sérgio. When I was very young, my family moved from rural Brazil to the big city of São Paulo. My parents hoped to find a better life for us in the city. We set up our home near other migrant families in São Paulo. We are lucky because we have enough food to eat and we all get to go to school. But some others are not so lucky.

www.heinemannlibrary.co.uk
Visit our website to find out more
information about Heinemann
Library books.

To order:
☎ Phone +44 (0) 1865 888066
🖨 Fax +44 (0) 1865 314091
💻 Visit www.heinemannlibrary.co.uk

Project edited by Briony Hill
Written by Lynette Evans
Edited by Lynette Evans
Designed by Steve Clarke
Original illustrations © Weldon Owen Education Inc. 2008
Illustrated by Mike Spoor
Picture research by Jamshed Mistry
Originated by Weldon Owen Education Inc.

Printed in China through Colorcraft Ltd., Hong Kong

Acknowledgements
We would like to thank the following for permission to reproduce photographs: Courtesy of Street Kids International/www. StreetKids.org (George, Zambia, p. 21); Getty Images (cover); Jennifer and Brian Lupton (students, pp. 22–23); Photodisc (boy, p. 2; p. 24); Photolibrary (homeless family p. 15; woman with stall, p. 20); StockXpert.com: Rodrigues (São Paulo, background, pp. 22–23); Tranz: Corbis (p. 1; homeless person, pp. 2–3; favelas and high rises, pp. 14–15; pp. 17–18; Gol de Letra programme, p. 19; homeless family, United States, p. 20; Philippines rubbish dump, pup tents, Paris, p. 21); Reuters (Brazilian president, p. 19; boy, Mumbai, p. 21); www.flickr.com (background, pp. 20–21).

ISBN 978-0-431179-69-8 (hardback)
13 12 11 10 09
10 9 8 7 6 5 4 3 2 1

British Library Cataloguing in Publication Data
Evans, Lynette.
    Rich or poor?: poverty and inequality. – (Worldscapes)
362.5-dc22
A full catalogue record for this book is available from the British Library.

Contents

Look for the **Thinking Cap**.
When you see this picture, you will find
a problem to think about and write about.

Unexpected treasure

The grand hotel

It was the fountain that got Isabel into trouble that day. She would not usually go near the lobby of the grand hotel with its polished marble floors, gilt-edged mirrors and shiny leather lounge chairs. But she had arrived at the kitchen doors earlier than usual that morning. The shadows of night still lingered, and the hotel was hushed as if sleeping. Isabel pushed half-heartedly at the door, and to her surprise it swung open. When she stepped inside, she could hear a rush of falling water. Isabel was quick and **impulsive** by nature. Before she knew it, she had followed the sound to the end of a twisting, dark hallway. She stood gazing at a shimmering curtain of water that cascaded from ceiling to floor. A huge fountain was shooting water skywards in a magical blend of light and colour.

Isabel scanned the lobby quickly. There was no one at the reception desk, and the security guard was slumped in his chair, snoring softly. Just as she was about to step out of the shadows towards the dancing lights of the fountain, there was a hustle and bustle outside the great glass entrance doors, and the guard awoke with a start. Isabel shrank back into the darkness, her heart pounding wildly in her chest. She watched as smartly dressed doormen appeared out of nowhere to welcome the guests inside. A boy and a girl who looked about 13 years old, the same age as Isabel, laughed as they entered the hotel with their parents following close behind. They tossed a football playfully back and forth between them.

impulsive acting on the spur of the moment

A close call!

Isabel shook her head. What a fool she had been to risk so much just to look at a stupid fountain. The little kids back at the **favela** would have bellies growling with hunger by now. And if the old cook in the kitchen was found giving away a bag full of day-old bread each morning, he might lose his job. In return for his kindness, Isabel made sure that other street kids didn't bother hotel guests by begging for handouts as soon as they stepped outside the hotel.

Isabel darted down the twisting hallway, trying to find her way back to familiar territory. She nearly jumped out of her skin when a wild-eyed figure appeared suddenly before her. Not being accustomed to mirrors, it took her a moment to recognise the reflection of the thin, agile girl with wispy, dark hair and fierce, coal-black eyes as herself!

Hearing footsteps, Isabel quickly rounded a corner and found herself in the hotel restaurant. The smell of sizzling sausages and eggs made her mouth water even before she saw the feast of foods before her. There were mountains of tropical fruits, platters of steaming pancakes and baskets full of freshly baked breads. Crisp, linen cloths covered tables that were laid with gleaming crockery and vases of fresh flowers.

To Isabel's horror, the footsteps drew closer, and she was forced to dive beneath the nearest table. The family from the lobby had arrived for breakfast. As luck would have it, the waitress showed them to the very table where Isabel was hiding! As soon as the parents got up to select their food from the buffet, Isabel heard the clatter of dropped utensils. She saw two smiling, inquisitive faces peering at her from beneath the tablecloth. 'Hi,' said the boy, 'I'm Rico. And this is my little sister, Zara. Why are you hiding under our table? Do you need help?'

favela settlement of shacks; often on the outskirts of a Brazilian city

6

Some people say that the term *favela* comes from the flower of a thorny plant that once grew wild on the hillsides where Brazil's first shanty towns were built.

Out on the street

Isabel didn't think that her rough life on the streets of Rio was anything she would ever miss. But at that moment she wished with all her heart that she could transport herself out of that fancy restaurant and back into the chaos of her home in the favela. To her relief, Rico and Zara seemed to be friendly and not at all inclined to alert anyone to her presence. As if to confirm the friendship, Zara's cap, jacket and shoes appeared miraculously beneath the table.

'Wear these clothes,' Rico whispered urgently. 'Zara's going to create a **diversion**. We'll get you out of here!' And sure enough, with the cap, jacket and shoes as a disguise and with Rico striding confidently at her side, Isabel marched back down the hallway, through the lobby, past the fountain and out of the front doors without anyone looking twice at her.

diversion something that takes your mind off something else

The poorest people in Rio de Janeiro have the best views of the bay from their homes high on the hillsides. Rich and poor enjoy the beaches side by side.

'You really saved my skin in there,' Isabel said, as she stood with Rico outside the hotel. 'If I can ever return the favour, I will. And if you want to see another side of Rio, visit me in the favela. Many tourists come to see the sights and sounds, but it's not wise to come on your own. I'll make sure you and your family are safe.'

Zara joined them outside the hotel. 'What's a favela?' she asked.

Isabel looked beyond the hotels, high-rise apartments and luxurious mansions that lined the street. She pointed up towards the mass of rickety homes that spilled down the steep slopes surrounding the city. 'The favelas are where the working class families of Rio live,' Isabel replied. 'We may not have as much money as the people in this part of town, but we are proud of our community. **Samba** dance began in the favelas. You can buy the coolest art there. And my school has the greatest football team ever,' she said, as she glanced at Rico's football with a grin. 'I'll bet we could challenge you to an exciting game!'

samba Brazilian dance of African origin; also the music for this dance

Surprise visitors

That afternoon, a sleek sports car sped away from the hotel district with a throaty roar. Rico and Zara had convinced their parents to go on a tour of the favelas, as Isabel had suggested. It wasn't long before the wide, paved inner city streets turned into narrow, winding roads. With every twist and turn, Rico's mum flipped and rustled the city map in a desperate effort to find the Tourist Centre. The brochure said that favela tours operated from the centre twice a day, and that some of the local children had been trained to guide tourists through the favelas.

'I'm going to have to pull over,' Dad said. 'We seem to be lost!' Rico and Zara peered out of the car windows as their parents tried to make sense of the map and their position. Suddenly, a gang of hollow-cheeked, barefooted children appeared out of the shadows and surrounded them. Then Rico and Zara heard a familiar voice.

'Glad you guys could make it,' Isabel shouted above the excited chatter of the children. 'Come on, we'll show you around, but leave your camera behind. Most people here don't like to be photographed!'

With their parents in tow, Rico and Zara raced to keep up with Isabel, as she led them through the maze of alleys and stairways in the favela. 'More than 50,000 people live in this favela,' Isabel explained. 'Some people here are so poor they have barely enough food to eat. But most people do at least have electricity, running water and TV,' she continued, pointing to the satellite dishes perched precariously on the corrugated iron rooftops. 'This community school has been built especially for us kids in the favela,' she said proudly. 'One of Brazil's most famous football stars helped build it. He even runs football workshops. That's why our team is tops! We're training for a big tournament next week, and we're about to have a practice session on the beach. Would you like to join in?'

Rich rewards

Rico's green eyes lit up with excitement, and Zara tugged impatiently on her mother's sleeve, asking for permission to join the practice session. Like Isabel and the other kids in the favela, Rico and Zara were crazy about football. They raced down the hillside with the school team and were soon kicking and chasing a ball with the others. The competition was fierce, but it was a friendly match, and both sides cheered when Isabel won the ball off Rico in a spectacular sliding tackle.

At home, Rico and Zara would have been wearing shin pads and soccer cleats, but here their feet were sinking into the thick, white sand of the Brazilian beach. With the famous Sugar Loaf Mountain as a backdrop, the children were having the time of their lives. It seemed to make no difference that Rico and Zara shouted out in English while many of the other kids shrieked encouragement in Portuguese. In the excitement of the game and beneath the same hot sun, their differences melted away. They all had the same goal in mind – fun and friendship.

Put on your thinking cap

Write down your thoughts so that you can talk about these questions with a classmate.

1. Why do you think wealth and possessions are not shared evenly between people in the same country or around the world?

2. Do you think it is fair that some people can have too much food, while others go hungry? Why?

3. Why might it be dangerous for tourists to walk around the favelas without a local guide?

4. Why didn't the differences between the children matter during the football game?

What's the issue?

Brazil is rich in natural resources. It is the biggest country in South America. Much of the northern part of Brazil is covered by the largest tropical rainforest on Earth, the Amazon. The second-longest river in the world, the mighty River Amazon, winds through it. Brazil is one of the most important farming countries in the world. It is a leading producer of coffee, oranges, soybeans and sugar. Huge supplies of nuts, timber and other products are harvested from Brazil's forests. Power stations along the rivers generate a great amount of electric power. Valuable mineral resources, such as iron ore, are mined from the land.

Brazil's productive **economy** has brought great wealth to a small number of Brazilians. Some own huge areas of land. They live in large mansions, beautiful country villas or elegant high-rise apartments. They travel in luxurious, chauffeur-driven cars. However, the wealth of a few contrasts sharply with the extreme poverty of most Brazilians. More than 50 million people in Brazil are poor. Some live in rural areas. Others live in crowded urban slums, called favelas. Many barely earn enough money to survive. The struggle to close the gap between rich and poor is one of Brazil's greatest challenges.

economy the system in which goods and services are produced and traded

Living on the streets

As a result of poverty, millions of children in Brazil have to work instead of attending school. They must beg, steal or work for long hours to get enough money to survive. Some of these children live in favelas, but many have no homes. They sleep in the streets, under trees, in doorways or on benches. Some have been left to fend for themselves by parents who are too poor to feed or clothe them.

Most of the time, these children do not have enough to eat. They suffer from **malnutrition**. Because of their poor diet, they can suffer from disease too.

In Brazil, the richest 10 per cent of the population receives about 30 times more income than the poorest 40 per cent. About 20 per cent of Brazil's population live on less than £1.50 per day.

malnutrition harmful condition caused by not having enough good food to eat

An unfair share

The unequal distribution of money, possessions, food, education, employment and health care is not a problem that affects Brazil alone. Some people in other countries enjoy great wealth, an excess of fine food, high standards of education, good jobs and the best health care the world has to offer. At the same time, large numbers of people around the world live in poverty. Many of the world's poorest people do not have access to safe drinking water, or to basic services, such as health care, **sanitation** and education. A lack of services makes it difficult for people to break the cycle of poverty and improve their lives or the lives of their children.

People in poor rural areas who are struggling to make ends meet often migrate to cities. They hope that in a busy, bustling city there will be enough work and money for all. In Brazil, the largest cities are São Paulo and Rio de Janeiro. At the edge of these cities, people have built rickety shacks made of cardboard, corrugated iron or wood on land that they do not own. These favelas contrast sharply with the sleek skyscrapers and modern high-rise buildings in the downtown areas. Some favelas are home to many thousands of people. Life in the favelas is tough, and the rate of crime is often high. However, many of these communities have a rich culture and energy of their own.

sanitation   systems for keeping water clean
and getting rid of sewage

Many of the world's poor make a living by sifting through rubbish dumps. The United Nations Children's Fund (UNICEF) tries to help children by paying parents the loss of a child's income if the child attends school.

Put on your thinking cap

Write down your thoughts so that you can talk about these questions with a classmate.

1. In many parts of the world, people suffer from health problems caused by overeating or poor food choices. Serving sizes are too large. Food choices are too rich. How could the world's supply of food be shared more fairly?

2. If children have to work instead of attending school, then they will not get the basic education they need to ever break free of poverty. People who do not have an education cannot get a job that earns a decent wage. How could this cycle of poverty be broken?

Rags to riches on a rooftop

Some of Brazil's most seriously underprivileged children are reaching for the stars on the rooftops of Rio! The Gol de Letra foundation has opened a new centre in one of the city's poorest favelas. Many of the children never attended school. Many never had an opportunity to explore dance, music, art, literature or sports. For these children, the opening of the centre marks the opening of a new world.

Brazilian novelist Jorge Amado once wrote that 'poverty is the absence of opportunities to develop one's own talents'. Former Brazilian football champions and founders of Gol de Letra, Raí and Leonardo, have taken these words to heart. In 1998, the stars founded Gol de Letra, meaning 'perfect goal', to help children living in the poorest favelas of Rio de Janeiro and São Paulo. Today, the centre helps more than 7,000 families.

Children in the Gol de Letra programme attend school for $3\frac{1}{2}$ hours each day. For each child, the project lasts for seven years. Gol de Letra has sister foundations in Italy and France that raise funds for the Brazilian projects. Gol de Letra has become a global model for breaking the cycle of poverty through education. Children also take part in music, dance and sports.

Fome Zero (Zero Hunger)

Brazil's president, Luiz Inácio Lula da Silva, is committed to ending poverty and hunger in Brazil. President Lula was born into a poor, working class family. His parents were unable to read or write, and Lula himself didn't learn to read until he was ten years old. He began working at an early age to help his family.

As a young man, Lula formed Brazil's Workers' Party and fought to improve life for Brazil's poor. When he was elected president of Brazil in 2002, the first thing his government did was establish Fome Zero (Zero Hunger). This programme provides food coupons and money for more than 11 million of Brazil's poorest families. It encourages poor families to send their children to school.

19

Despair and hope

Homes into hostels

BRAZIL – A growing number of favela residents in Rio de Janeiro are creating small businesses and turning their homes into hostels to give tourists a taste of the 'real Rio experience'. For many tourists, this is a chance to invest in the lives of Brazil's poorest families.

The land of plenty?

UNITED STATES – Although the U.S. is one of the world's richest countries, the level of homelessness and hunger is growing. An estimated 12 million children live in poverty. Food banks, soup kitchens and homeless shelters are stretched to the limit.

Slums demolished!

INDIA – Homeless people in Mumbai (Bombay) paid good money to a landlord to fill swampland and put up shacks. In no time, a shanty town grew. Six years later, machines came to tear the illegal homes down. Where do the poor go now?

Street Kids International

ZAMBIA – When George's parents died, he was forced to live on the streets. Then Street Kids International came to the rescue. Through SKI, George was able to get some business training and a loan to set up a street stall to support himself.

Dump of despair

PHILIPPINES – People living in shanty houses on the edge of Manila's largest dump were caught in a rubbish slide as rain brought the mountain of rotting waste tumbling down. The dump is a means of survival for the city's poor, who search through the rubbish each day for something to recycle and resell.

Pup tents for the poor

FRANCE – There are an estimated 86,000 homeless people in France. But for a lucky few in Paris, there is now welcome shelter against the biting winter winds. In the midst of this elegant city, more than 200 tents have been donated in an effort to help the homeless.

What's your opinion?

In many countries around the world, the gap between rich and poor is growing. When it comes to meeting basic needs, such as having a safe and clean home, food on the table, shoes and clothes to wear, a school to go to and access to good medical care, some people are bombarded with a wealth of choices. But other people have few, if any, choices. Today, nearly half of the world's six billion people live on less than £1.50 per day. Many children are forced to work simply to survive. Many of the world's poor live in **makeshift** shelters in slums and shanty towns where crime rates are often high.

- Do poor people have a right to build makeshift homes on land that is not theirs? Why or why not?

- Should children be allowed to work to help support their families, even if this means that they miss out on school? Why do you feel this way?

- Do governments have a responsibility to ensure that all children have enough food to eat and access to basic education and health care? Explain your answer.

- Is it fair that the rich often seem to get richer, and the poor poorer? Why or why not?

makeshift   made from whatever materials are available, and usually to be used for only a short time

I don't think children should have to work for a living. All children should be able to go to school and have the chance to be a kid. If they have to help support their family, they should be allowed to work for only a few hours a day, after school.

I think that poverty is a problem that affects everyone in the world, even rich people. I don't think people in some places should be stressing over which brand of cereal to buy, while others die of hunger. We are all responsible to help end world hunger and poverty.

I don't think it is fair that some people can build houses illegally on land they did not buy. When one person does that, others follow, and shanty towns grow out of control. It is not safe for the people living there and shanty towns look ugly. Governments should provide safe, low-cost housing for poor people.

Think tank

1 Imagine that you won a million pounds. What would you do with your money?

2 If you had the chance to be mayor or prime minister for a day, what would you do to help struggling families in your town or country?

3 Do some research to find out which countries in the world have a small gap between rich and poor. Which countries have a big gap? Which countries have been most successful in closing the gap?

Do your own research at the library, on the Internet, or with a parent or teacher to find out more about poverty and what people around the world are doing to help others in need.

Glossary

diversion something that takes your mind off something else

economy the system in which goods and services are produced and traded

favela settlement of shacks; often on the outskirts of a Brazilian city

impulsive acting on the spur of the moment

makeshift made from whatever materials are available, and usually to be used for only a short time

malnutrition harmful condition caused by not having enough good food to eat

samba Brazilian dance of African origin; also the music for this dance

sanitation systems for keeping water clean and getting rid of sewage

Index